The Calling of Your True Self

The Calling of Your True Self

Elizabeth Anne Bell

ATHENA PRESS
LONDON

The Calling of Your True Self

ISBN 1 84401 754 0

First Published 2006 by
ATHENA PRESS
Queen's House, 2 Holly Road
Twickenham TW1 4EG
United Kingdom

Printed for Athena Press

My Own Knowledge of Life and Death

*M*y name is Annabella. I have what I call psychic intuition, clairvoyance and medium-ship. I can speak to people who have passed over – over the fine line, as I call it. It's a fine line in my mind as I believe we revolve in a circle, living and then leaving for a while. The fine line divides us from those who have passed over to another level, and that is why we can still be in touch with those we love: because it is a fine line.

I have read tarot for more than twenty-five years but it was not the first thing I did. As a child, something instinctively told me that people did not die, they just went to another place for a while till the time was right to come back into another body, but your soul remains in the new body of your choice, when it is time to return. We don't die: we are all spiritual beings so our real home is when we leave the earth plane until it's time to come back into a new body, same soul. That's why getting in touch with your true self – the spirit side (which we all are) – will make you see through different eyes. Remember, your eyes are the windows of the soul. Heard that saying before? Of course you have, we all have. Where did it come from, nobody seems to question; we all come out with spiritual sayings. These sayings come from the spirit within, the true self. We all repeat these proverbs, but do we think about why we say them? It's time to tap into your true self.

In my eyes, you don't die.

This belief is what drew me towards reading cards. I also do psychometrics and hold certificates 1 and 2 and a master's degree in reiki healing, but the first thing I ever did was a Ouija board when I was only nine years old. This does work, but you can attract bad energy – I know: I have done it. I advise anyone to have a medium, someone who knows what they are doing, present when doing this, as it is not a game: some lost souls will attach to you if it is not done properly. Always light a blue candle and an orange candle and have a bowl of water with three drops of sage oil added. All these things protect. I will tell you about this later in the book.

I did sort of leave the spiritual world alone when I left school for a few years. Then when I was twenty years of age I was drawn to the spiritual church.

Today I do tarot and act as a medium. I get in touch with people who have passed over and give clients the names of their loved ones, how they passed over and tell them things only they could know. I can tell them what the deceased looked like. To me, the way to explain is that it's like a television in my head and spirits tell me things but you have to understand the symbols they give you. Sometimes it's not explained too clearly.

I also do reiki healing. I feel drawn to healing and helping people as much as I can. If you are drawn to the spiritual and want answers, *read this book:* it will open the light within you, helping you to make your thinking patterns different, making your life easier.

The power of your mind is up to you.

About Myself

My real name is Elizabeth Anne Bell. I had a near-death experience at the young age of eighteen months old. Being too young to remember myself, my knowledge of this was given to me by my parents.

I was on the danger list for eight months. My dad had to give me the kiss of life while waiting for the ambulance. He said my eyes rolled to the back of my head and I stopped breathing. He said he can remember the day I came home, 'And the only way I can explain it is you looked like an angel.' He said I was looking around as if I didn't know what was going on, he said he felt he was looking at a different person: 'You looked serene.'

I do feel this is where it all started…

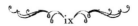

Contents

I: Understanding Birth and Rebirth

I feel life is a circle, being born and reborn. I really believe we are all here to learn. It's school in a way, but we take too many things for granted. If, for example, something does not go right in your life you should not just walk away because you can't cope; you have to face up to your problems. Only *you* can take control of your life, only *you* can make the change.

Every day of your life on this earth plane was planned before you were reborn again. Only some people who have completed their life on earth will remain in the other world, as they have learned all they need to know. They will be your guide in life, from your birth until you die; they remain with you always.

I have knowledge from my spirit friends

that you carry over into your next life what was not completed in your last life, and therefore you are drawn to certain things and people in your life for a reason. You choose the family you want to be born into. You are doing this, remember, before you are reborn, as you have powerful recollections of what you were like in your lives before, and this is why you choose who will be your parents.

Before we are reborn, we are shown what I will call our own 'journal' of all your lives. Your journal is proof of all the lives you have lived. It is kept safe in the spirit world. Everyone has one. You will add to your journal. On your return, your new life will be shown to you before your return. You won't remember your journal when you begin your new life, but your life, remember, is already written. And throughout your life you will be drawn to certain places and people, you will choose certain things for your home. All these are meant for you: it's all a sign from a previous life. That's why you may feel more comfortable with some people than others.

Your subconscious is your spirit side: your conscious mind only wakes this up now and then, without you knowing. Your subconscious holds the key, and you can tap into this through meditation.

In each life cycle, you have to go through hard times. If you try and run away from what I call your destiny, you will prolong things and make them harder. It is hard to understand why you have to go through so many bad things in this life. You only have memory of this current life because when you are reborn, your subconscious withholds what happened in your past lives, but sometimes you do feel like you have been somewhere before when you haven't; or you meet someone and feel comfortable with this person. Well, it is for a reason you are put together; you don't know why, but something tells you it is so.

Has your life never changed through meeting someone? Of course it has. It happens because it's your pathway: some things are good, some are to wake you up.

I believe you go into your new body just before you are born. I feel if you leave it too long to enter the body or change your mind – and I do feel this happens – or you have been stopped as your guide changes his mind and wants to delay it for a good reason, that is when a child is stillborn and is taken back because it was the wrong time for them. It seems very hurtful for the parents but this person was going to be you and then it was decided it was not right and it was planned this way till the last minute. That is why sometimes doctors can't understand what went wrong.

I used to ask myself, Why bring a child into the world only to take it away? But I was told it was not the right time or a mistake was made or the soul went to the wrong body: it makes sense to me, but it is still very hard for the parents. Remember, their destiny has been planned also and they knew about this before they were born, but again it is buried in the subconscious and they don't have any recollection of these events.

I believe life is worked out for everyone. You must have said to yourself when you are having a bad time or things keep going wrong, 'Why me?', 'What for?', 'What have I done to deserve this? I must have done something wrong in another life.' So why did you say this? It didn't come from nowhere, it is what was stored in your subconscious before you were born again. Things like this slip out now and again because we are all spiritual, and now and again, we are given the odd sentence to remind us that we have lived many times before.

Some of us listen, some don't. Those who do will be guided more fully in their current incarnation.

When a loved one leaves us very young as a child, or as an adult who dies unexpected, it was planned. As hard as it is for the person involved, the person was taken for a reason; it was planned for them to return to get ready for another incarnation.

I fully believe people come back into their own family again when a child is born. Again, I put to you another saying: when a child is starting to talk and communicate, most of us will say, 'He's been here before.' Ask yourself why do you say this. *You must believe in other lives*. It's not a saying: it's your subconscious opening, just a little, your spiritual side – we all have it, but we don't listen to it enough. Don't be afraid of it, it is there to help and guide us all.

I also believe we are reborn male and female but come back as one sex most often. I feel if you come back and were not happy being male or female and wanted to stay the same sex every time you are reborn, that is where genes get mixed up and when we are reborn into a sex we are not happy with we become lesbian or homosexual, or like both sexes. It's not the person's fault, or the parents': *it's the way that person was meant to be*.

I also think that when a child is born with the personality of someone other than the parents it's hard to cope with and understand. I feel they were very angry at life when they left this world. On their return, that anger was carried over in their karma; their colours are wrong in the aura and they still have lessons to learn. They are put with the parents of their choosing before they were reborn. I feel the parents have still got lessons to learn also, and that is why they choose each other; but remember, you have no recollection, so when your life is turned upside down without any reason, or you ask yourself 'Why?' what answer do we all come up with that we have all said at some point in our life? 'What have

I done to deserve this? I must have done something wrong in my last life.' Well, it's right, but you can start to put things right. That is why you need to listen to your intuition, but I will tell you that later on.

II: Your Inner Voice

We all have an inner voice. Some of us listen to it and some of us don't. What you have to do is go with your instincts – most of the time, but not all of the time. If it feels really strong you will know. If you feel torn with a decision you will get an unpleasant feeling if it is not the right one. That is your inner voice telling you to hold with your decision, wait a while longer, the time is not right, you will be making a mistake. On the other hand, if you have a good feeling, then go for it. Your inner voice is your spiritual guide and we all have one.

We are all born into this world with our own guide. It is up to you to listen. If you listen hard enough, you'll get answers, just ask from your heart and really *mean* it. You must know what I am saying: you know that you talk to yourself and then answer yourself back

– we all do this. This is why I am saying listen to your inner voice. You are not answering yourself back: it's your guide's voice, listen to the tone.

But you don't realise, you don't know how to get in touch. We can all get in touch. Hearing your own voice is your higher self. A male voice is an angel or guide; your family or friends sound the same as they did when in body. Sometimes you will get a tune in your head and won't seem able to get rid of it. Take notice, as this is also guidance trying to tap into you, from the spirit world.

Meditation will open the door.

Meditation is being inside your mind for ten to fifteen minutes.

You need to go to a quiet room and be on your own. Go to a place in your mind. What makes you feel happy and relaxed? You must really put yourself there. It must be a calm place, you must block your mind to any other thoughts. This may take a few weeks to master. You need to write down what – or who – comes into your mind. It is very important if they give you anything, as these are symbols for you to remember, and each time you have time to yourself you will know the same person by the symbol. This is your guide who gives you symbols. You may get colours or a star – anything. It may just be a quick flash *but write it down*. This is their way of coming through. You may get a clear picture in your head of a face or what they look like, what they are wearing; you may even get a name, but don't worry if names don't come, it is not important. Ask a question then listen for the answer. Write down the first thing you think you hear and keep all your notes. You will at first think it is you answering yourself back. Give yourself time on your own, just fifteen minutes two or three times a week. After a time you will know the difference between your own voice and your guide's.

You must want to do this; it does not come without thought. You have to close your mind just for a short time.

Your guide could be an Indian chief, a priest, a doctor – anyone. That is why I ask you to write down your first impressions when you look inside.

All the things you are drawn to in life are brought with you when you are born again. You may be in a job you are not happy with; something is telling you to make a move as this is not what you should be doing. Some of us just keep doing the same thing because we are frightened of change; instead of making the change our inner voice is telling us to ignore it. If a feeling is strong and it is telling you more and more every day, *you must do something about it.* This is your inner voice. It is time for new challenges and this is where your life is meant to go. If you ignore these things you will make yourself ill as stress will kick in and play havoc with your body. What your inner voice is telling you is a must. You are getting back a feeling, and it is time to listen and change your life.

I will just give you an instance with your work and stress. If you are in a relationship and you are not happy with your work, you get stressed and take it out on the person you love most and end up in arguments and you don't understand what is going wrong.

It is not your relationship that' wrong, it is your work. This is why I ask you to listen to your inner self. If you are not happy with something, change it. I also feel if you don't listen you could end up losing the person you love, which happens so often for the wrong reasons.

We are all spiritual beings: if you ask for help you will get answers.

Another thing I would like you to listen to is your dreams. Everybody dreams, but some people don't recall their dreams. I ask you to keep a pen and paper by your bed and start making notes as most of your dreams are telling you something important.

Look for strangers in your dreams as people you do not recognise are guides coming through to give you a message. Loved ones who have passed over will come into a dream and let you know that they are still there. Take notice: this is their way of communicating; they are really there, that's why it feels real.

It is just a fine line that separates us from the other dimension till it is time to reincarnate. You're only cutting the cord of life till it's time to enter your new body with the same soul.

What is important is to listen to your inner voice.

When you get the feeling something isn't right don't confuse it with everything that goes wrong in your life all together, or you could end up throwing the wrong things away. Ask for help in your dreams but be patient as the answer could take time.

I often have dreams that come true. I also dream of loved ones and friends who have passed over. Some of my dreams have helped me make really good moves in my life; that's why I ask you to write your dreams down. Loved ones come into your dreams as their spirit, they are really there in spirit – that's their way to connect.

I lived abroad for twelve years. I had a really strong feeling from my mother, who had only passed away two months earlier, to return to England. My dream was so vivid and colourful I just knew it was a message to go back. I will give you this example just so you know what I mean about interpreting your dreams.

My mother-in-law has also passed over, and in my dream they were both there. I was in a garden. My mother-in-law was planting seven plants, but the last one was perishing. I pointed it out to her; she told me to water it and it would be all right. She then turned to me and said, 'The seeds are already planted, you will flourish on your return.' She disappeared and my mother tapped me on the shoulder. When I turned she was holding a Union Jack flag.

I know the seeds my mother-in-law was planting were for me; the Union Jack was my mother telling me to go back to England. I did return and I have not looked back...

Everyone at some time gets a feeling that something is wrong with either family or friends and you have the urge to make a telephone call. You do this and find out you are right and it makes you feel strange inside. You must have had this experience. Again, it's your inner self, your guide, giving you information.

So if you want to be in touch with your

inner self, I will teach you how throughout this book.

We have all done things with mixed emotions and felt really bad afterwards. It's called making the wrong move, but the thing is, when you have done this you know something is telling you it's wrong and sometimes you take no notice. You feel torn between which way to go and picking the wrong way is called a lesson we have to learn – learning the hard way. But you had to go this way to be where you are today, so in a way it felt like a bad move at the time, it felt bad inside, but you were pushed this way for a reason. Having said that, you choose your path, *only you*. It's up to you now to put it right. Sometimes it means putting your move down to your own misguidance; it was a move to make you look at your life. You can be wrong but you will be brought back to where you are supposed to be if you misguide yourself.

If you can relate to any of these things I have mentioned you are on your way to opening the door to what you were born with and everyone is born with, only some of us want to learn about it and some don't.

Only you can open the door to the light within. When you do you will feel more at peace with yourself.

It will take time and patience, but remember *it is already there.* You are the only person who can wake up the spirit within, and when you do your life will run a lot more smoothly and the things you found hard work before will become easier as you will start to see things in a different light and to approach things in a different way.

III: Being in Touch with Who You Are

When I meditate I see strong colour as a symbol. This may take time, but don't give up if it does not come to you right away.

We need to be aware of energies around us, other people's energy. You will be fascinated once you tune in. Our body is like a radio: we need tuning in, and you will, believe me, if you persevere.

Before starting any meditation I ask you to surround yourself with a gold bubble. Just imagine being enclosed in this colour and in your mind ask this light to protect you at all times. The bigger you make it the better. Ask for good energy to surround you. After finishing say thank you for this protection.

The room you choose must be calm, so

switch off phones and if anyone is in the house ask them not to disturb you for twenty minutes at least. You can play some music to relax you, but keep it low. You need to do some breathing exercises to relax you, so first lie down with a pillow under your head. Breathe in deeply right into your stomach and hold for thirty seconds, then release very slowly, blowing out. Repeat three or four times then empty your mind and just go inside yourself. Imagine being somewhere peaceful, imagine sitting at the edge of a gently flowing stream. Look into the stream. As you throw a pebble into the water, watch the ripples. You may get patterns or shapes; write down what your impressions are. You may look to your right and see someone walk towards you – ask who they are, ask a question and see what comes back, go with your first answer. Ask them to sit by you, notice everything around you.

Open your hands to this person you see and press your hand into theirs. As you do this, take a deep breath and feel the energy being passed, then breathe out gently. You may feel a tingling or a warm feeling; this means you're connecting. When you feel ready, open your eyes, take another deep breath and release. Get up in your own time and thank the universe for the energy you felt or received.

You may even see a loved one who has passed over when you meditate, a flash in your mind: it's not a flash, it means you are getting in touch. Just little things at first mean you are using your spirituality, which we all have. Some can tap in; some of us block: it's all down to believing there is more to this life. There *is* afterlife, there is no end.

Your dreams are also signs. Listen to them and write them down. If you see a stranger in your dreams this could be your guide coming into your dream to give you information; write it down – things that seem so silly in your dreams may be important.

Another good form of meditation is colour. You must learn there is an inner child in all of us and this will help you to get in touch with your higher self. Your higher self is who you really are. If you learn to tap into your higher self you will begin to see life at a different level and understand why certain things happen in your life: it is all for a reason.

To do this, I want you to sit down again in a quiet place with your feet firmly on the ground. Put both hands on your knees, palm up, and press together your index finger and thumb. This helps you connect in your mind. I want you to ask for any guidance from your higher self. Ask three times, always saying thank you. Clear your mind, close your eyes and imagine your higher self twelve inches above your head. I would like you to image the colours red and orange. Bring these colours down into the crown of your head; you must really think strongly. These colours are streaming through your crown then to a point between your eyes. If this is working you should feel some kind of pressure. Now bring the colours into your throat, then slowly into your heart. Send love from your heart, with these colours still flowing into your stomach then into your lower stomach. Now move the colour gold down to seal these colours in. Take deep breaths into your stomach and hold for twenty seconds then breathe out slowly. Really imagine these colours flowing into every cell in your body. When you feel ready, open your eyes slowly. Take one more deep breath and hold, then gently breathe out slowly. You can now get up and get on with your day. You should feel energised. This really helps to give you more energy if you do it twice a week.

Each night just before you go to sleep, ask your guide to show himself in your dreams, speak to him, ask him questions – see what answers you get. This will take a while to master, but don't give up; if you believe from your heart, you will get answers.

We all get down when things are not going our way or not moving fast enough and start to take it out on people we love most. We end up making the wrong moves, through wrong thinking, instead of going inside and getting in touch with our higher selves. When asking your guide for answers, ask him to touch you in a certain place for a 'yes' and a different place for a 'no' answer. Close your eyes and still yourself. Ask the angel of your choice. I do this, and I know the different touch from angels, guides and my family. My mum's touch is a tingling on my lips; my guardian angel is itching on my face and chin. These sensations are a sign for you that they are there. Some signs are like fine hairs, as if you want to touch your face to move them. It can also feel like cobwebs, as if you've walked through a web itself. My life guide brings with him a strong feeling on the crown of my head, as if something is stroking in a circular motion. My healing guide is Red Indian and I feel a strength around my shoulders and pins and needles down my arms when he's around.

We are all looked after. Don't press the self-destruct button when you feel low: we must learn to listen. Start doing these meditations: they really do calm you. For instance, I want to talk about anger. We get angry mostly with the people we love. When our emotions are all over the place, we lash out not knowing what for. Sometimes you don't think straight when you are angry, so never mix your emotions and anger together.

If you are making an important move in your life, emotions do strange things to your thought pattern. What I am saying is *don't let it take your energy*. Lots of things around us every day can play havoc with our emotions.

They can draw negative energy to us, causing all sorts of problems. This comes from people you never thought would send it. If someone sends bad thoughts out towards you, you pick up this bad energy. That is why sometimes you feel on a downer and your emotions are all over the place and you don't know why; it could be negative energy being sent to you, but you can get rid of this with colour.

Once again let me remind you: *being around people who are angry does rub off.* If you are happy, you will make other people happy; if someone is sad, you will be sad: you rub off on each other, but keeping things locked up won't solve anything.

If you are unbalanced in your emotional centre you can bring on so many problems. Your stomach will be a number one target: if something upsets you or you hear bad news you feel sick, you feel like someone has twisted your stomach round in knots. This means you are turning your own energy round in the wrong direction and it brings you down. *Only you can change this,* again with good thought patterns.

All I am saying is that you must get rid of

bad feelings and you can. If you keep your feelings blocked you are blocking your system and you will bring illness upon yourself. Learn the colour technique and you are on the road to better health *and* better relation-ships with loved ones and friends.

IV: Colour your Aura Back to Positive Thinking

*Y*our aura is very important; you make your own aura. If you are thinking bad thoughts you are making murky colours in your aura. If you think good thoughts you will lighten it.

For instance, if something is going wrong with your work, family or relationship, your aura will become dirty. If you are depressed or stressed, angry inside, feeling empty, tearful or even holding back tears from your past from bereavement you will compromise your aura. Locked in anger is dangerous. It will lead to depression and stress. This will change your personality and lead to wrong thinking, making mistakes then wondering why things are going wrong in your life.

You must cleanse your aura with colour,

but I must stress to you that if you are feeling really bad and everything seems really black you may need professional medical help, then start to work with colour, as it does really work, but it takes time. Always ask for these colours to be rayed down and tell the universe what colours you want.

You can use colour for so many things, and once you master colour manipulation you will want to tell your friends. I mostly cleanse my aura with colour before I go to sleep or first thing in the morning. You must block all thoughts, you must bring the colour through the crown. You are fetching this colour from the universe, from your higher self, the transpersonal point. The chakras are your seven points – this is the spiritual you. If any of these points are blocked you can unblock them with colour and you must move these colours though each point, starting with the crown then to the point between the eyebrows, then your throat, down through your heart (there are two points here), then on to your stomach, just above your navel, and your lower stomach. Hold the colours in each point, feel the colour, feel the colour touch you.

With a lot of practise you will feel movement as if something is been lifted.

I have told you about orange and red; these are powerful colours. I personally use these colours a lot. They are good for stress if you move silver afterwards to all points. Always finish with gold to seal in colours. Don't worry if you don't feel anything straight away as it takes time; it will still work even if you don't feel anything – the sensation you should feel is a strong rushing feeling, a sort of light-headedness or pins and needles. I normally get a strong rushing feeling and feel it going from one chakra to another. Please remember to start this with your eyes closed. Move the colour through your crown, starting twelve inches above your head. Really concentrate on the colours. I feel a tingling feeling at the crown. If you don't feel this at first, don't worry; just take it to your third eye. This point is strong, the point between your eyebrows. Hold for one minute and then move to your throat, hold, and then to your heart.

Really imagine these colours wrapping around your heart as this is where you send all your love from. This is important and the universe will sense this.

Then move the colours to your solar plexus, just below your heart, then your lower stomach. Leave it there for a while longer as this is where we all hold so much stress. After you have done this, relax and learn deep breathing, which helps take stress out of the body. Just take a deep breath to the count of four or five – whatever you are comfortable with – and hold, then let it come out slowly to the same count. Do this three times. Imagine letting go of all the stress as you breathe out.

There is a saying: 'Be careful of what you ask for because you may well get it.' I am sure you have heard this saying. Well, there is a colour you can do this with and the colour is turquoise, but you must never do this to harm anyone. When you use it, do it from the heart; feel the colour wrap around your heart. But firstly you must visualise your desire in your head, as if you're making your own movie, but think carefully; first plan it, write it down and make sure happiness comes into it. Everyone daydreams about the things they want; well, your thinking goes to the universe, and the spirits do hear you.

Putting turquoise though you speeds up the process of attainment. You must not tell anyone what you visualise or you will break it. And once done, put it to the back of your mind and forget it. Thinking about it will delay its coming to fruition.

It is a scientific fact that distant healing works; self-healing, mind and body, also works.

Try this, but you must believe in your mind that you are cleaning your aura. Send your thoughts inwardly to every cell. First close your eyes and imagine the colour white descending from eighteen inches above your head, coming down though your crown. First into every cell in your brain enters a bright white light, radiating outwards, vibrating. Then move down to your third eye, the centre between your eyebrows. Imagine pure white light pulsating, vibrating. You may feel a rush in this area, as if you're being lifted, as this is the strongest point. Now go down to your throat and do the same. Stay on each point for three minutes: next your heart, then your stomach. This may be held for a while longer as we all hold a lot of stress in this area. When all your chakras are covered, imagine the white light vibrating throughout your whole body.

To finish always surround your entire aura with gold light as strong as you can.

This is a must as it protects your aura from unwanted energies as these energies can come from all directions, mostly when you are feeling low; other people can actually send bad energy. It's a good idea to do this twice a week and it will start to protect you right away.

V: Reiki Healing and How it Works

R eiki healing is universal. I have my master's degree. Reiki is a way of activating, directing and applying natural energy, promoting healing and balance. It helps and prevents imbalances, bringing natural healing powers; it releases stress and encourages total relaxation.

A treatment will restore energy. Reiki is love, the most powerful healer; when you feel unloved or alone, reiki opens your mind. It supports and helps in the medical profession.

I feel people are taking more responsibility today for their own well-being. It's time to recognise what reiki is. It is universal: it is life force. When you hold degrees your secret symbols are drawn from the universe into your energy field. Once a recipient is empowered with reiki they will have it for the rest of their lives. Reiki works on your mentality and emotions, touching into any imbalances before they manifest into disease.

All of us are life force.

Reiki comes from the healer's hands, through heat and energy. The healer tunes into universal energy: it's like tuning into a radio.

The reiki healer will draw her symbols into your energy field. This will create light to unblock any bad energy. As a reiki master I ask for spiritual help, I ask spirits to help in my work, to take the pain to the light with love. I mostly feel my Indian guide, or as I call him, my healing guide. I know he is there, as different clients have experienced his presence and told me the symbol only I know. I ask all my clients what they see while having reiki, as it does overcome obstacles they may have held for years: it's like shifting a big load from your shoulders, as the saying goes. *Reiki is a wonderful healing therapy.* You have to experience it to appreciate it; if you don't try you will never know. All it can do is clear you out; it can only make you better.

I was drawn to reiki because of health problems myself, having suffered with neck and back pain. Taking tablets for the pain didn't seem to take it away and the stress of it all led to a lot more ailments. I started suffering from migraines, dizzy spells and sinus problems, which in the end cause more stress.

I found out that one of the clients who I did tarot and clairvoyant readings for on a regular basis was a reiki master: Pat Cole, based in Tenerife. So I went for treatment and Pat encouraged me to take it up myself. I found the treatment really worked; I do healing on myself, three times a week, and no longer need painkillers.

I want to explain to everyone out there who suffers from any kind of ailment what reiki is. So many common ailments are brought on though stress. Stress causes blockages; blockages cause illness. We build these blockages up throughout our lives, from childhood to adulthood. I include childhood for many reasons: one is the way we are brought up. If, for instance, you had a bad upbringing –

which can be bad in many different ways —
you build up more blockages.

Maybe your parents argued a lot. If this was
the case then this can bring on emotional
problems causing you to withhold your feelings, which can cause blockages in the chest
or throat area: maybe you have asthma that
developed later in life or throat problems. If
you suffered rejection stomach problems can
be the result; abuse can cause depression;
violence can cause headaches; fear, arthritis:
the list is a mile long.

What I am trying to say, or get people to
understand, is that reiki is hands-on healing,
from head to toe, starting from the top and
dragging all bad energy, that has perhaps built
up over many years, out through the feet.

You may feel heat, and the pain can be
brought to the surface. You may feel the pain
in your weakest area becoming stronger: this
will subside; it's drawing the pain out.

Reiki can give you emotional release.
When you do your degrees in reiki you have
to memorise your symbols, as these symbols
can only be giving to you, by the master, who
has to hold the third degree, which I now

hold. I actually put symbols though my clients that are universal. It's a spiritual process; old emotions are brought to the surface, so in a reiki healing session you will get flashes of your past. It's for good reason: to release any bad energy. There could be tears as it's releasing the emotions you have blocked, perhaps for a long time.

The effects of reiki can change your life, ridding you of all those past emotions, but reiki cannot activate without atonement.

Reiki is a very ancient energy. You are not allowed to show the symbols to anyone.

There is no danger in reiki: it can only do good – I know, I am guided by my healing guide, who is a Red Indian. Many people who I have healed have told me afterward they had visions of a Red Indian and also my symbol (which only I know).

Reiki is a spiritual experience for the client as well, which calms and relaxes. You may have powerful dreams afterwards, which again is cleansing. I also ask you to drink plenty of water and drink no alcohol that day as it can have an effect.

Reiki can also be done from a distance when you have your second degree; all you need is a photo and candles.

The only thing I will say is that if someone comes as a total non-believer they will create a block.

Reiki can also be used to clear negative energy. I really believe a lot of us hold this without knowing, most of it from past experiences. It may appear out of the blue and bring on depression or even a breakdown. When you are that low you attract spirit attachments.

I can use my symbols to clear bad energy from a person or rooms that don't feel good, by burning sage oil – no more than six drops – and an orange candle. This will cleanse a room, asking light to be sent to every corner of the room. Ask for any bad energy to be taken to the universe, to the light with love.

Reiki is enlightenment. It comes from the universe.

Your emotional feelings are you: if your emotions are all over the place, your soul is suffering. Heard the expression 'Poor soul'? We have nearly all said this at some point, whether it be inwardly or out loud. What do you do automatically if you have pain? You rub it with your hands.

We are energy.

The healing is given to you from universal energy. Where do you look when you are feeling down, and ask for help? Up above. Think about it: you are a spiritual being, that is why you do it, but I really believe a lot of us don't even question why we come out with sayings and look above for help. You know why? Again, it's an inbuilt ability from being born but we ignore it. Reiki is like a light being turned on.

The energy comes from the universe. When I make contact through my hands the energy flows. Each attunement increases positive power to channel, so the reiki master has her body cleared of any obstructions, increasing the life energy from the universe. This is a very positive power; it is ki energy. This has now entered the healer's aura and clears all blockages; her seven chakras are being cleared. The reiki three masters' and teachers' degree is spiritual healing: it increases my ability to channel.

I was spiritual before I did reiki, but I now feel it has made this side even stronger. Reiki will go to any part of the body it needs to go to; it acts on anything that is there – disease, allergies, headaches. Reiki deals with the cause that brought on the pain in the first place.

Heard the saying 'Got to get to the root of the problem'? Your roots are your feet. That is why I always end a session by drawing the bad energy you have collected out through your feet to ground you.

If you want to come out of the dark into the light, believe in reiki.

Mandala

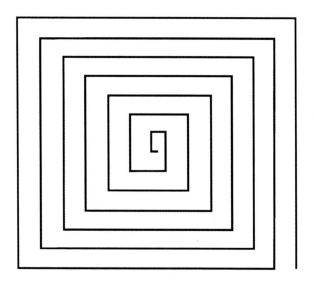

❧ Focus on the centre of the diagram.

❧ Continue to stare at the diagram until it splits into two – as though you are experiencing double vision. Don't take your eyes off the centre.

❧ Move your head three inches back and look at the whole mandala. You should start to see a colour.

❧ Look at the Colour Chart over the page to see what your colour means.

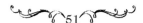

Colour Chart

RED
A sexual person full of zest, you have an inner strength, courage and self-confidence but could suffer with the stomach area as you hold grudges and block this area. You need to cool your anger.

ORANGE
Oranges are thrill-seekers who like a challenge – you need excitement in your life must. Watch out for back problems.

YELLOW
Fun-loving free spirits, you are wonderful to be around. You bring joy to others. You are an earth person and like nature, meaning you're not really suited to living in the city. Yellows can be shy and sensitive and are animal lovers.

GREEN
You are intelligent and process information easily. You have a good imagination, great ideas. You don't waste time and power

comes easily to you —you are a born leader and strong willed. Nobody will win an argument with a green!

BLUE Blues are loving people who live from the heart. You are very spiritual and make good teachers or nurses. You love to help others and are good listeners but can be very emotional. You could suffer with throat problems.

VIOLET Violets are leaders, tuned in to the inner self – both knowingly and unknowingly. You make good actors and are musical, but you need to meditate. You want to know about your life purpose and feel the need to connect.

LAVENDER You are a spiritual being, but also a daydreamer. However, daydreamers can turn their daydreaming into reality.

INDIGO You are at peace with new energy, living in harmony. You have high awareness and are very honest, highly intuitive, psychic people; old souls who know where they have come from and were born with spiritual memories. Most children are indigos – listen to these children: they hear and see spirit. Indigos are ying and yang, nice calming people to be around.

VI: Guardian Angels

*G*uardian angels are real. We all have one or more. They *do* protect; they feel your pain. They *do* know what you are going through. I really know the difference between an angel's touch and that of my guide or loved ones who have passed. Their touch comes through in different areas of your body.

You may feel itchy, mostly on your face and the crown of your head, like a fly is crawling on your scalp, a feeling of cobwebs on your face. I have had some strange experiences but now I know why and what they are all for. Just a few years ago I was rushed to hospital as I was experiencing bad migraines and also sinus problems. I had brain scans and they all came out clear. I was still getting all these symptoms and getting nowhere with the doctor's help. I really felt strongly that I was blocking some part of my spiritual self and therefore creating my own blockages and causing these symptoms. I also knew it was spirit trying to get through. The truth was, I was getting cracking and popping noises in my nose; these are again more signs of angels and spirit energy trying to connect. So I was determined to clear this and decided on reiki healing, which I picked up straight away. The heat and pain coming to the surface was instant; I knew then it was going to clear as I was getting a wonderful feeling of protection, and I knew the messages I was receiving were real.

The angel's touch is soft and gentle, on the left side of my face. Virtues are angels who listen to your prayers and then healing energy is sent from the universe. Ask for it to be sent from your heart to the person you want it to be sent to, the same way for yourself. Afterwards thank your angel three times: there is something about the number three that they like.

Archangels Michael, Gabriel, Auriel and Raphael assist us all in everyday life. Invoke one of these angels to help you, just before you sleep or early in the morning. Always ask from your heart. Angels love the colour pink, so imagine this colour as you send out your thoughts to the angel of your choice. Light a pink candle, but remember to put it out after you send your message. Your birth sign will tell you which is your archangel:

- ❧ MICHAEL: Aries, Leo and Sagittarius. Element: fire. Colour: red.

- ❧ GABRIEL: Cancer, Scorpio, Pisces. Element: water. Colour: emerald green.

- ❧ AURIEL: Taurus, Virgo, Capricorn. Element: earth. Colour: white, earth tones.

- ❧ RAPHAEL: Gemini, Libra, Aquarius. Element: air. Colour: blue and gold .

Anything fragranced with rose will attract guardian angels, as well as rose quarts crystal.

I want you to still your mind. To do this you must not have any distractions, so it's best done when you are on your own.

I want you to close your eyes. Take a deep breath into your abdomen. Count to three slowly, and hold. As you are doing this, imagine your eyes rolling to the third eye, your third eye being in the centre of your forehead between your eyebrows. Breathe in through your nose – breathing through your nose is very important as it activates the third eye. Breathe out through your mouth. Slowly do this three times, then invoke your angel, inviting him down beside you. Ask from your heart. Anything you need help with, your answer will come soon if you believe from your heart.

When you are finished, thank your angel. Then imagine pure white light around your entire body, glowing seven layers deep. Imagine pure white light vibrating outwards. This will protect you. Do this often enough and you will set up a barrier, as I call it. Just letting good energy, positive energy into your aura protects you. Protecting yourself is very important. You can also do this with gold, which is also a very protecting colour. Tipping it with a blue outer line makes it even stronger.

All things that happen in your life are for a reason, even if it does not feel fair at the time. For instance, do you know someone who had a lucky escape from an accident, or so they thought? Did they say, 'It must have been my guardian angel looking after me'? Why do we say that? Think about it, it happens all the time. We as humans think it was a miracle.

Another saying: 'What a miraculous escape they had today.' We are looked after, all of us; we all have guardian angels. If our time is not up in this life, we will have 'miracles', as we think if then, as it is not our time yet. So believe in your guardian angel.

Another saying: 'God moves in mysterious ways.' Well, he does, as it was meant to be – another saying: 'It was meant to be.' You must have heard someone at some time say that. Well, that's because it *was* the time.

I think that when strange things happen it's the energy calling you to listen.

Listen to your thoughts, as thoughts give answers. Why do we question ourselves when we want answers? Where do you think it came from – *your* answer, I mean? Your inner thoughts are answers from the universe: they are your answer most of the time.

Your guardian angel and your guides are

invisible, if you want them to be. If you open up to touch and the angelic realms you will begin to find life easier. I believe we say all these common sayings without thought. *Ask yourself where they come from*. Again, it's locked in your subconscious, but your spiritual side will slide into your conscious mind now and again without knowing. That is why I know we are all spiritual beings.

When we start to look inside for answers we will find life much calmer and our thoughts will be answered, as they are not just our thoughts: our guardian angel is always in our thoughts and they know when we are hurting and are there to help us all.

Don't be afraid to ask for help.

Your guardian angel is always there: it's just like picking up the phone when you learn to tune in.

Learning to tune in to your guardian angel comes through patience and learning to shift your conscious mind to your subconscious. Your subconscious is your spiritual side, the awakening of your true self.

Again I would like you to think about popular sayings. There is more to them than words: they're all linked to the universe, where we are all from, where our real home is. We are here for a good reason; I think the reason is to put mistakes right, but some of us keep doing the same things over, then wonder why things keep going wrong. They are going wrong because we are not learning, we have blinkers on.

When things go wrong another saying is: 'Out of something bad, something good will happen.' What is really happening is it's time to shift, time to move on. It may be a difficult choice at the time, but it is your guardian angel at work, shifting you to where you're meant to be, and believe me they are right by your side. I want you to look back to when things have not been good, just for a split second, and look where you are now.

The word 'angel' comes from the Greek *aggelos*. Angels can incarnate into human form. Heard of the saying 'She's an angel'? Where did it come from? Your subconscious. Your subconscious is your spiritual self; I believe the soul carries all knowledge to the next life, but we are not allowed to know it all, just a snippet here and there is all we are allowed. That's where the saying 'She's been here before' comes from: because we all have, only we are not allowed to know all from a previous life as it would be too mind-bending.

So what I am saying is that nearly always out of something bad something good will happen. *Remember to ask your guardian angel and believe.* You are looked after: your guardian angel is at your side always.

VII: How to Tap into your Sixth Sense

We all have a sixth sense. You would not be reading this if you did not believe there was something more, but your sixth sense lies dormant if you want it to. It's up to you to tap into it; again, it takes time and meditation. We are all born with a sixth sense, but unfortunately we do nothing to awaken it. Your sixth sense will be woken up through your own will power (again, power we all have).

Your sixth sense comes through dreams, thoughts, gut feelings – you must have had a feeling about whether you should do what is on your mind or not; you get a good feeling or a bad feeling. Sometimes we make wrong decisions in haste or fear; doing this means we are not tapping into our sixth sense.

I am not saying everything will come up roses by using this sense: what it helps with is not making a rash decision. It's called *listening*. Listen more to your own feelings and take time out before making very important decisions in your life.

Mediation is the call, the calling to your awaking. A good book on mediation is by Ted Andrews. He is a very good author. I have read most of his books. I have studied for years about angels, guides, meditation, tarot, dowsing, medium-ship, crystals reading and photographs.

Your sixth sense is already there, it's up to you to open it up. When you learn to tap in you will start to lift barriers you did not know you had. You will feel better, coincidences will occur; this is to move you to where you are supposed to be.

You can programme your mind to tap in to your higher self. Your higher self is the real you, the spiritual you: tapping into this will provide guidance coming through dreams or coincidences.

I call roadblocks in your life the wrong job, the wrong relationship: these will make you feel uneasy and your health will suffer. Think now, are there roadblocks in your life? A man or a woman in your life or a general bad feeling? This is called a gut feeling or sixth sense.

You can change this.

Have you heard the saying 'He's seen the light'? Well, that's what your sixth sense is; you will see the light, but it has to be through meditation. Your sixth sense is your thoughts. Your subconscious can bring things back to your conscious mind and help you make the right moves.

You must have on occasion met someone and felt it right: it was fate. What do you think fate is? Fate is your destination, where you are suppose to be. That is why we meet certain people at certain times in our lives, when we are supposed to. To change your life examine your thoughts. Our thoughts control our minds. Are your thoughts deep? If they are, it means you are on your way to tapping into your sixth sense.

Learn to cleanse – cut off from all that has clung to you all day. At work you have been around people with bad auras and this will rub off on you. You must have been around people at some time and felt uncomfortable: people with good auras will think of other people most of the time before themselves, and are nice to be around. Your sixth sense is picking up on this; sometimes you can help the person who carries so much weight or walk away till the time is right. Carrying too much weight means you're clogging your charkas and this can make you ill. That's why tapping in can lift the weight.

You must have heard the sayings 'Carrying too much weight', or 'It's like a weight being lifted from my shoulders'? It's true: a lot of illness is brought on through unnecessary worrying, and also, as strange as it sounds, people's bad thoughts toward you attach to your aura and penetrate it. That is why sometimes you may have an off day, feel down and not know why. This can go on for a long time if you don't cleanse it; that is why tapping into your sixth sense and meditation can really help turn your life around.

Your sixth sense is when the phone rings and you know who is on the other end or you're thinking of something and a partner or someone close picks up your thoughts. That happens to most people but they put it down to coincidence. What is a coincidence? Have you thought that out? No, probably not. It means you're tapping in. Have you ever changed your mind as to what you are going to do on a day off and found with the change of mind, it changed your direction, or you met someone you have not seen for a long time? Well, it was meant to be. Your thoughts are your sixth sense: you were meant to be there.

Ever heard the saying 'I was in the right place at the right time', or 'I was in the wrong place at the wrong time'? Sometimes we miss a train or a bus or even a flight, and something happens – there is an accident. You were not meant to be there. Think about all these things that have happened in your life. At some time your life has turned in another direction, even though at the time you didn't want to go somewhere, you went and you met someone and ended up with their phone number, kept in touch. That person was meant to come into your life. Think right now: who is still in your life connected to you by some random exchange of phone number yet you are still in touch. It was meant to be.

Some people stay in your life if they are meant to; if they are not doing your life purpose any good, you will either change your direction in your life or you loose touch: that is for a reason.

Again your sixth sense will guide you if you listen. Right now I would like you to close your eyes. As you do, imagine looking upward, but centring your attention on your third eye, the point between your eyebrows. This should really have an effect like a pulling feeling. Ask any questions and listen to the answers. This may take time but believe me, it works. After you have done this, cross your legs at your ankles, rest your hands on your legs and press your thumbs together. Imagine a golden bubble around you. Let it enter every cell in your body. This keeps you protected and grounded, which is very important in any spiritual work you do.

Everyone at some time in their life will get an uneasy feeling when around the wrong people. It may be someone you have known for a long time or even a stranger. The feeling is a gut feeling: that is why we all say at some time 'I have got a gut feeling about this.' The gut feeling may be a job you're doing. You have a feeling you need to change your direction, or the place you live; something is telling you to move on. It may be the biggest decision you feel you have to make at the time, but you just know you have to do this.

I want you to look back at these times and then look at what changes it has made to your life now; it may have really changed who you are now, made you value people more. It's very important to love yourself and it's important to respect others and treat them as you want to be treated. That is why listening to your sixth sense is attending to the real you. Go with your instincts when they feel strong, because believe me they will take you in the right direction, even if it is very painful at the time, it will lead you to where you're meant to be.

When you begin to tap into your sixth sense you will feel a lift, a feeling of peace within. As your guide is always by your side it's a safe feeling, a feeling of self love, of learning who you are. Learning to love your-self is a great gift to yourself. You will find your life changing for the better as you start to bypass the negativity in your body that no longer serves a purpose. You will start to think more positive thoughts.

VIII: Psychometry: Learn to be in Touch by Touch

Psychometry involves holding an object or a piece of jewellery in your hand. You could try this with a friend or partner. Take something from each other and hold it in your hand. Sit facing each other, now close your eyes, take some deep breaths and release slowly. Do this three times, and relax.

Empty your mind and think clearly of a colour of your choice. Now concentrate on that colour and nothing else; anything that pops into your mind will mean something, even if it may feel like nothing. If you get flashes of anything, tell the other person. You may get names, you may see someone, you may get a place: this is a start to linking into your sixth sense.

When you do this it is best to light a blue

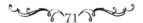

candle, which protects and draws spirit. Having a crystal next to the candle will heighten its power.

Using this as a way to touch is something that will not come in an instant: you must be patient. It also works if you take the item home. Hold it in your own space and have a pen and paper ready and write down what comes into your head. Take a photo of someone, you can pick up on this also. It really works.

I remember my first experience with psychometry. I was twenty-three years old. I took a photo in my hand and held it for about two minutes. At first I felt a coldness in my leg, then a gentleman told me his name was Thomas. He was sitting with his leg in a dish. He gave me a cap – it was a soldier's cap. He told me he was the uncle of the person who gave me the photo. I saw this in my mind's eye – it's called mental medium-ship. I was then told he was a soldier and was shot in the leg and the only relief he got was putting his leg in a dish of warm water. Afterwards, the lady who'd given me the photo told me this was indeed her uncle.

Finally, I want you to make sure you always protect yourself in all spiritual work. It is very important to do this all the time: if you don't, you can draw unwanted energy to you without knowing, which in effect will drain your energy. It is very easy to protect yourself, and the more you do this the stronger the protection will be. It will become automatic.

How to protect is simple. I want you to close your eyes and imagine there is a golden beam of light extending twelve inches around you, outwards and upwards. Feel it vibrate like a fan, then finish as if it is a big circle right around your entire body. This is your shield; make it your shield. Every time you do spiritual work, always thank your guide and your angels when your finish your work.

My afterword is:

Believe the energy around you; believe you are loved.

Angels are there instantly if you call: it is no trouble at all to them; they are there to protect and help at all times. Remember, every single person is special; don't put yourself down; you must tell yourself you deserve love. Open up to the messages from your angels. The light is within everyone. If you call in the light you will find peace and your true worth in life without fear.

Remember, tuning in takes time and patience, but fear will disappear from your life and be replaced with love. Remember, the universe is only an appearance superimposed on the transcendent reality. The soul is the higher mode because it is conscious spirit: it is unconscious ready to be awakened.

IX: Epilogue

Remember to tune in. To tune in is to switch off. Switch off your conscious mind. Tune into your subconscious. Meditation is the light within tapping into your subconscious, your true spirit.

Say one affirmation a day: say to yourself, 'I am love, I am loved, I send love.' Then send the pink light of love to someone you care about or want to help. Imagine deep rose pink going from your heart to theirs (doing this really works). It's really good if you've had disagreements. Sending out light will touch their soul. You will find more love coming from this exercise.

Ask your guardian angel a question. Your answer will come in some form, be it a dream, a vision, a thought, a phone call, a direction change. You may be reading a newspaper and some article will send a thought out to your mind (all the things you do come from thought). Remember, thoughts are our way forward. Some of us are not aware that thoughts are sent from the universe. You must have said to someone or even yourself, 'I just had a good idea.' Your idea was sent through a thought. Messages are sent from your guides and angels, and these are all signs from the universe, *the calling of your true self.*

Lots of light and love.

Appendix – The Chakras

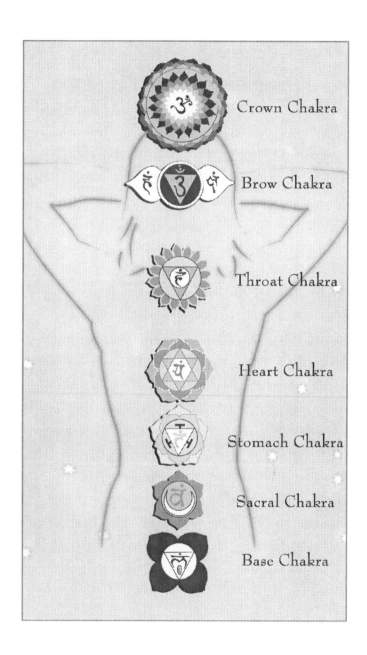

Crown Chakra

Brow Chakra

Throat Chakra

Heart Chakra

Stomach Chakra

Sacral Chakra

Base Chakra

	Colour	Scent	Stone
CROWN		Lavender & Frankincense	Clear
BROW		Juniper & Rosemary	Purple
THROAT		Chamomile & Eucalyptus	Blue
HEART		Rose & Ylang Ylang	Green & Pink
STOMACH		Chamomile & Eucalyptus	Yellow (inc. Turquoise)
SACRAL		Jasmine & Sandalwood	Orange
BASE		Patchouli & Geranium	Red & Black

Musical Note	Element	Sense
B	Spirit	Esp
A	Electrical	Sight
G Sharp	Spirit & Air	Sound
F Sharp	Air	Smell
E	Fire	Taste
D	Water	Taste
C	Earth	Touch

Printed in the United Kingdom
by Lightning Source UK Ltd.
121070UK00001B/74